Shelter

Being an intentional parent
in a random world

by Jimmy Holbrook

randall house

114 Bush Rd I Nashville, TN 37217
randallhouse.com

Shelter

© 2009 by Jimmy Holbrook

Published by Randall House
114 Bush Road
Nashville, TN 37217

Front cover design by Daniel Kraeer, www.danielkraeer.com.
Cover photo courtesy of Stefania Barbier, Rome, Italy
Author Photo for back cover courtesy of Laurie Rhodes, Shutterbug Photography, www.shutterbug-photo.com

Printed in the United States of America

10-ISBN 089265578X
13-ISBN 9780892655786

www.randallhouse.com

I would like to dedicate this book to my parents, who provided me a Shelter of development and the Focus on the Family Institute for changing my life. Last, but not least, this book was made possible by the people in my own Shelter; Abby, Joel, Jonah, Faith, Katelyn, and Zoe. I love you!

Table of Contents

Foreword

Parenting is tough work. Anyone who argues with you has never had children.

Someone once said that when a couple has their first child, they're able to protect their child with a two-on-one defense. Once the second child arrives, the parents are forced to move to a man-to-man defense. If the loving parents are blessed with a third little one, they'll spend the remainder of their lives in a zone defense.

As a parent with six children of my own, I've always chuckled at that analogy. All laughing aside, when God trusts a child to our care, we're given one of the most serious responsibilities we'll ever have—raising a child to know, serve, fear, and love Christ.

I don't know many parents who aren't crazy about their kids. Sadly though, the burdens and busyness of daily life often quietly and subtly lull us into a tranquil and passive state of parenting. Instead of consistently painting a biblical vision and direction for the next generation, it is so easy to coast down the road of life without our hands on the wheels of parenting. When trouble inevitably arises, it is all-to-easy to suddenly "over correct" with bursts of anger and frustration.

There must be a better way.

My oldest daughter was about three years old during one of the busiest seasons of my life. While serving a church as an associate pastor and attending seminary full time, I found that I was home less and less. One evening I affectionately told my firstborn, "I know Daddy's been busy, but I'll be home tonight to tuck you into bed and kiss you good night." She peered at me with her big blue eyes and innocently said, "But Daddy, you don't live here. You live at the office."

Her words changed my life forever.

After significant life changes, I'm still seeking God to become the parent God wants me to be. And more so, to raise my children to become everything God wants them to be. That's one of many reasons I'm excited about *Shelter*.

Jimmy Holbrook clearly understands and masterfully articulates the mandate parents have to provide a biblical shelter for children from the distractions and temptations of this world. As a parent of five children. Jimmy shares his valuable real life experiences intermingled with his years of serving faithfully as a pastor.

Some advice about families and parenting seems too lofty to achieve. Some books on this subject are difficult to follow and understand. Jimmy's work and advice is neither. Laced with personal stories and easy to apply principles, Jimmy will challenge you, love you, and walk with you as a fellow struggling, yet faithful and sincere parent toward God's best for your kids. His down to earth—yet scripturally rich insight—is sure to touch your heart and direct your future.

I know it has mine.

Recently I had a moment with my son Sam that I'll treasure forever. Dreaming about his potential future, I boldly asked my budding eight year old, "What do you want to be when you grow up?" Sam beamed with pride as he replied, "Daddy, I want to be what you are!"

Glowing with pride I replied happily and somewhat surprised, "You mean you want to be a pastor like Dad!" Sam shot back with great enthusiasm, "Nah! I said, 'I want to be what you are! I want to be a great daddy one day!'"

As you prayerfully read and experience *Shelter*, I'm confident you'll become even a greater mom or dad.

Introduction

May 8, 2003 is a day I will never forget. I cannot recall how my day began, but I vividly remember my journey home as if it happened yesterday. Stuck in traffic on the interstate, I thought I heard a storm siren. Motioning the passenger in the vehicle next to me to lower his window, I asked, "Dude, is that a storm siren I hear?" "Yeah man, the radio just broadcast a tornado warning!" The look on his face told me we were thinking the same thing, "This is not good!"

Turning on the radio I heard the weatherman warn, "If you are in the path of this storm you need to seek shelter immediately!" He pinpointed the location and I was directly in its path. Fortunately, the traffic began moving a little faster. About two miles farther and I could exit east and get ahead of this storm. Those two miles were the most stressful miles I have ever driven. The skies blackened and it began to rain. When I tried the windshield wipers, they did not work. Unable to see, I missed my exit! My only recourse was to go to the next exit and back track.

All I wanted to do was just get home, but I wasn't making much progress. There I sat, staring straight at a wall cloud. I grew up hearing about wall clouds but this was the first time I had ever come face to face with one. What I had always said I wanted to see was about to take place.

A cone dipped out of the cloud and descended

midway between the surface of the earth and the wall cloud.[1] Dirt and debris violently shot up from the ground to meet the cone, forming a perfect funnel. Right before my eyes a tornado was on the ground less than a mile away and headed straight for me. Quickly I looked for a place to seek shelter, but there was nothing. The tornado was directly behind me. I smashed the accelerator to the floor and headed straight for my house.

I have never been that scared before or since. When it was all over I went outside alone and wept. I don't ever want to see a tornado again. That day I got as close as I ever want to get!

A shelter would have changed this experience for me. Instead of running I could have entered a shelter and been just fine, although danger was all around me. If you are a parent, you are raising kids in a dangerous culture. This book is not about sheltering your kids from this danger, but focuses on building a shelter of development in the midst of a dangerous culture. That is exactly how God develops His children. He personally teaches His disciples how to love Him with all their heart, mind, and soul, while providing the protection of a divine shelter. Jesus does not take us out of this dangerous world when we choose to follow Him. Rather, He develops us in the midst of the danger, teaching His warriors how to recognize truth and live meaningful lives.

We should treat our families the way God treats us by giving them the opportunity to develop underneath the protection of a family shelter. Throughout this book I refer to the family as a shelter. In Deuteronomy 6, God gave humanity His divine design for the family. The

---

[1]Most strong tornadoes form within wall clouds.

family is a shelter where warriors are developed and the truth of God is transferred to the next generation. I am passionate about inundating the next generation with truth and challenging them to be in the world but not of it. My intent is not for you to isolate your kids from our dangerous culture, but that you will be challenged to intentionally develop fierce warriors *FOR* a dangerous world. Join me on a journey where you'll discover how to teach your kids that Christianity is not what you do; it's who you are! It's not just a decision you make; it's a lifestyle you live!

Jimmy Holbrook

Chapter 1

The Divine Design

Developing a Healthy Vision for Your Family

Family Vision

Sometimes when I think about my wife and children God gave me, it just blows me away. I have been married to Abby for 12 years and we have had five children in the last seven years. The creation of the family is incredible and has enormous value in the eyes of God.

Why did God create the family? For many it could be summed up in two words: Bed and Breakfast! But certainly God had more in mind than mere survival and economics. In the Genesis record we gain insight into the infinite wisdom of God as He creates the first family.

> *The LORD God said, "It is not good for the man to be alone. I will make a helper suitable for him." . . . For this reason a man will leave his father and mother and be united to his wife, and they will become one flesh* (Genesis 2:18, 24).

Man was created in the image of God, and was not designed to live alone. Therefore, God created woman,

15

and when the two unite before God, they are no longer two, but one. From the first family to my family and yours, God sets His eyes on the transformation of two people into one family.

What is so incredible about this truth is that the family is also a place of creation.

> *So God created man in his own image, in the image of God he created him; male and female he created them. God blessed them and said to them, "Be fruitful and increase in number; fill the earth and subdue it. Rule over the fish of the sea and the birds of the air and over every living creature that moves on the ground"* (Genesis 1:27-28).

God chose the family as the vehicle through which new souls would enter the world. When that new soul, created in the image of God, enters the world, it is not designed to be alone. Therefore, God places this soul in a family. God's purpose for the family is the development of the soul. You and I have an incredible opportunity to develop a soul for the living God of the universe!

Great families do not happen by accident. They require discipline and commitment. Discipline and commitment are difficult to maintain without vision. *Where there is no vision, the people perish* (Proverb 29:18 KJV). Without proper vision, you and I are not able to maintain the proper discipline required to develop our families for Christ. However, when we share God's divine vision for our families, we can achieve incredible results. Andy Stanley coined the term *visioneering* in his book with the same title. He writes, "Visioneering is the course one follows to make dreams a reality. It is the process whereby ideas and convictions take on substance." If I were to boil it down to a formula, it would look something like this:

When we have biblical vision for our families, we are inspired and convicted to take action with a sense of determination to complete what God started.

I was born and raised in central Oklahoma, commonly called "Tornado Alley." Every year, without exception, when spring rolls around it brings severe weather with it. It is not uncommon to have your favorite television program interrupted with a tornado warning and the weatherman advising you to seek shelter immediately. At this point, with the sirens blaring and five children from infancy to seven years, it is all about organizing chaos and getting everyone into the storm shelter.

That's just the way our lives are. One moment everything is calm and the next instant a storm blows in, seemingly out of nowhere. God designed the family to provide shelter during these unpredictable storms of life, which is precisely why you and I must have a vision for our homes to function as Family Shelters. Read carefully the words of Moses as he communicates to Israel God's vision for the family.

> *These are the commands, decrees and laws the LORD your God directed me to teach you to observe in the land that you are crossing the Jordan to possess, so that you, your children and their children after them may fear the LORD your God as long as you live by keeping all his decrees and commands that I give you, and so that you may enjoy long life. Hear, O Israel, and be careful to obey so that it may go well with*

---

[1]Stanley, Andy; *Visioneering: Fulfilling God's Purpose Through Intentional Living*, Multnomah Publishers, (1999), Page 8.

*you and that you may increase greatly in
a land flowing with milk and honey, just
as the LORD, the God of your fathers,
promised you. Hear, O Israel: The LORD
our God, the LORD is one. Love the LORD
your God with all your heart and with all
your soul and with all your strength. These
commandments that I give you today are
to be upon your hearts. Impress them on
your children. Talk about them when you
sit at home and when you walk along the
road, when you lie down and when you get
up. Tie them as symbols on your hands and
bind them on your foreheads. Write them
on the doorframes of your houses and on
your gates* (Deuteronomy 6:1-9).

This passage leaves no doubt about God's purpose
for the family. It is to be a place where His values are
transferred to the next generation. You must see your
family as a shelter of development for Christ. As you
create this family vision, three elements should make
up your family shelter.

Safe House

Extreme windstorms caused by hurricanes and
tornadoes in many parts of the country pose serious
threats to buildings and their occupants. To protect
themselves, some homeowners choose to build safe
rooms. These rooms are generally closets inside the
home that are solid concrete, reinforced with steel. The
purpose of a safe room or a wind shelter is to provide a
space where you and your family can seek refuge that
provides a high level of protection. An outsider would
never know a home did or did not have a safe room until
a violent storm hit the house. Then and only then would
the vision of that homeowner be revealed.

If we have no vision for our families to be safe houses, our spouses and children have nowhere they can go to seek refuge. Solomon, the wisest king who ever lived, taught us, *He who fears the LORD has a secure fortress, and for his children it will be a refuge* (Proverbs 14:26). A man and woman with a healthy view of God worships Him, and that reverence alters their behavior. It motivates them to make the wise decision to construct a shelter that serves as a refuge from any type of storm.

Different storms cross our paths much like winds that are propelled by the jet stream. Sometimes it is the storm of change. Our lives are constantly changing. We often have to change jobs, houses, schools, and friends. When the storm of change blows through, we need a shelter, a place that remains constant in our lives. God has ordained the family as that place of stability.

Another storm we will face is the storm of failure. Everyone in your family is going to experience failure and that includes your kids. Mark it down; it will happen! So when your children come home, they don't need their parents on them for not doing better. Children should certainly be challenged to excel, but the time to challenge them is not in the midst of failure. The challenge phase should have already taken place. When your kids fail, they experience pain with their peers. If the world tells your children they are failures, and you tell them they are failures, eventually they believe they are failures. We often speak without thinking, adding to the overwhelming sense of failure. Building safe houses requires hard work. Recognizing the need for safe houses enables us to provide homes for our kids that help develop strong warriors for God.

Life is going great and then out of the blue rejection hits. This storm will happen in your teenager's life over and over again. They need the security of knowing their home is a place they can go without fear of rejection.

The challenge with this storm is if you are the one being rejected by your teenager. I know she does not like you. She thinks you are stupid and a nerd. He hates your rules with a passion, and you often argue about them. That is all normal and part of adolescence, the way most teenagers think, which does not require discipline. Even though your kids think all of those things, and they never tell you how much they appreciate you, the day is coming when they will. I used to think all of those things about my parents, but today I am so thankful for the experience they gave me. Words cannot express how much I appreciate my mom and dad today because no matter how much rejection I experienced in my life, I never experienced rejection at home. It was always safe!

God hates divorce and the pain that comes with it. Because of divorce the place of acceptance becomes the place of rejection. The shelter God designed becomes the eye of the storm. As a parent, nothing is more important than building a safe home. Endure whatever rejection you may experience from your kids and focus on maintaining a safe house. Your children worry about everything; grades, the opposite sex, making the team or squad, losing a friend, their face breaking out, wearing the latest name brand, getting braces, how many friends they have on Facebook, and the list goes on. They want to come home to a safe place, even if they never acknowledge it. They will one day, so Mom and Dad, keep your house safe!

Green House

We live in a day where it is popular to "go green." Recycling is in vogue, SUV's are going out and hybrids are coming in. God has entrusted us with the task of being good stewards of the earth. It is something we need to do better than we have done in the past. But we also need to make our families green, and I'm not referring to recycling.

The Bible often compares the family to a garden. *Let our sons in their youth be as grown-up plants* (Psalm 144:12 NASB). The family is a place of growth, a garden in which to grow people. God brings a man and a woman together, creating a family. Then the process of growth with the birth of our children begins. In the last seven years God has given my wife and I five plants (kids). Abby says, "He's done!" These plants are growing up in our home. Our responsibility is to take care of them, and it is hard work to keep this garden free of weeds. We are the ones who will speak truth into their lives and expose them to God. We tend to them and develop them into the people God wants them to be.

The fruit they produce with their lives has a great deal to do with how well we manage their growth. They are plants in the garden God has given us to grow. Our responsibility is to take them through the proper stages of development and lead them into the Lordship of Christ. We will discuss this in a later chapter. For now, Mom and Dad, make up your mind to build a green house. Plant your kids and grow them for Christ.

Fun House

Your home should also be a fun house, a place where you kick back, relax, take it easy, and enjoy life. The challenge here, especially among Christ's followers, is that a lot of homes get so caught up in the green house effect that parents operate like drill sergeants. Avoid the trap of being so consumed with turning your home into a learning center that it is no longer fun. Once again, if we turn to the wisest king that ever lived he tells us, *"Enjoy life with your wife, whom you love."*(Ecclesiastes 9:9). I saw a bumper sticker once that read, "The family who prays together stays together." I would certainly recommend that you pray, but if you fail to play, they won't stay! Why would a kid want to come back home later in life if he never had fun there when he was young? He won't, and that is why you must develop a vision of your home being a fun house. Be intentional and have fun with your kids. They grow up faster than you realize. Read them *The Chronicles of Narnia* and watch their eyes burst with anticipation. Take your little boy outside and play a game of dodge ball. You'll be amazed how much fun it is to whack your kids in the head with a rubber ball. Do it once, and they will beg you for more. Teach them how to wake board, take them hunting and fishing, sit down for a nice cup of make-believe tea, wrestle, tickle them, laugh with them. They are a gift from the Lord.

> *Behold, children are a gift of the LORD, The fruit of the womb is a reward. Like arrows in the hand of a warrior, So are the children of one's youth. How blessed is the man whose quiver is full of them; They will not be ashamed, When they speak with their enemies in the gate* (Psalm 127:3-5 NASB).

I am increasingly aware that my kids are only here for a season. Enjoy every moment with them and make sure your home is a fun house.

May 3, 1999 was the largest tornado outbreak ever recorded in Oklahoma. I listened to the roar of one tornado as it destroyed my friend's home. As soon as I could I went to check on them. It was like a war zone where a bomb had exploded. Trees were sheared with only the trunks sticking out of the ground. Boats and campers were on top of houses, and cars were rolled up like aluminum cans. Fortunately, our friends were unharmed, but many were not because they had no shelter from the storm.

On a recent flight home I sat next to a scientist who is a professor at the University of Oklahoma School of Meteorology. He shared a fascinating statistic. He said it was amazing to him that only five percent of homes in the state of Oklahoma, "Tornado Alley," have storm shelters. Only five percent are ready for an unpredictable storm to hit their home in the middle of the night. It is troubling to think about the risk so many people are taking with their families. When the unexpected happens, and the storm approaches, my family and I only walk a few steps and are safe inside our shelter. What is more troubling for me, after 17 years of ministry, is the risk people take with the spiritual development of their families. I know storms are approaching every human being on this planet. It is not a matter of if the storm will hit your family, it is a matter of when the storm will hit. Don't leave your loved ones in a vulnerable position! Adopt a divine vision for a family shelter that offers refuge for when the unpredictable storms of life come crashing in.

Chapter 2

Only a Warrior Can Develop a Warrior

Comprehending the Developmental Process

First-Hand Experience

Having vision for a family shelter is important, but it is not enough. Providing a shelter where your family can develop requires that you have first-hand experience of having been developed within a family shelter. You may be thinking, "It's hopeless! My childhood was horrible. I have no idea what it is like to be developed within a shelter that provides protection from the storms of life." No doubt, having parents who provided a solid family shelter is a tremendous advantage, but that is not the first-hand experience that is so important. What is important is the first-hand experience of a divine shelter in your life. It is the name of the Lord that provides that divine shelter. Solomon wrote, *the name of the LORD is a strong tower; the righteous run to it and are safe* (Proverbs 18:10). The Lord is our refuge and it is to Him you must go if you are to provide a shelter for your family.

Only a warrior can develop another warrior, and it is through the family that development takes place. The family is the primary vehicle through which God transfers His values to the next generation. God did not ordain the government, the school, or even the church to accomplish this task. It is the parent He has chosen, and it is a high calling indeed, one that you can not fulfill if you have not been transformed. Christ came to take ordinary people like you and me, transform our souls, and use us to accomplish extraordinary things to change the world one warrior at a time.

To become one of Jesus' followers a person must first experience a spiritual birth. While talking to a man named Nicodemus, Jesus said, *I tell you the truth, no one can enter the kingdom of God unless he is born of water and the Spirit. Flesh gives birth to flesh, but the Spirit gives birth to spirit* (John 3:5-6). If only a warrior can develop another warrior, then what does Jesus do? He personally develops warriors through the power and presence of the Holy Spirit, transforming us from the inside out. This is the divine transformation that enables us to gain first-hand experience of what it is like to develop in a safe, green, and fun shelter.

Identity

The re-creation of the soul brings a new identity in life, one that begins when we experience the incredible love Christ has for us. Life is no longer about what we do or achieve. It is about who we are in Christ. The Spirit of God is now living in us and allowing us to develop underneath the umbrella of His protection. When the storm of rejection blows into our lives, we now have a strong tower to run into for safety. God is constantly developing us spiritually so we are able to fulfill His purpose for our lives—God's objective since the beginning of time. King David, who was used by

God to defeat Goliath and lead the nation of Israel, is an excellent example of God using people to fulfill His purpose. Psalms are a peek into David's personal journal of spiritual development. King David shows us what it is like to go through development with the protection of a divine shelter.

The Four Phases of Spiritual Development

When you surrender your will to Christ and undergo transformation, you occupy an incredible position.

> *Do you not know that your body is a temple of the Holy Spirit, who is in you, whom you have received from God? You are not your own; you were bought at a price. Therefore honor God with your body* (1 Corinthians 6:19-20).

God dwells in your life, giving you the power to do what you could never do in your own strength. When the Spirit of God moves into an individual, He takes the person through four phases of spiritual development. The apostle Peter lays out the biblical model for this development in the second chapter of his first letter to the church.

Infancy

The first phase is infancy. During this phase of development an individual starts to crave the truth like an infant craves milk. Anyone who has spent any time around a baby understands this concept. Although an infant has not developed a vocabulary, he or she is extremely effective at communication. My daughter, Katelyn, will wake up in her crib and cry out until someone addresses her needs. Her mother will go to her and ensure that her needs are met in order to sustain her life.

People go through this same process spiritually. The crises people face in their lives often brings about spiritual birth and causes them to crave nourishment for their souls. They cry out, and God provides His Word to bring nourishment and comfort to sustain them through their time of trouble. During this phase people deal with spiritual questions such as: "Who is Jesus?" "Who am I?" "What is the meaning of life?" Once a person acknowledges that Christ is indeed God in the flesh who died for the sins of the world, that individual experiences spiritual birth, recognizing that Jesus is the way, the truth, and the life.[1] This recognition of truth creates a spiritual appetite for more truth, and so begins the process of spiritual development.

Construction

Following infancy the newborn believer enters the second phase—construction. You and I are living stones that are being built into a spiritual house for God. God is changing us to be more like Him, and while that is being accomplished, we bring glory to His name. At this stage we begin to look more and more like Christ. Now is the time to move away from the milk of the Word and feed on the meat of God's truth. As we digest the truth from the Scriptures, a change takes place, manifesting itself outward and which reflects the glory of Christ. It is during this phase we begin to discipline ourselves in order to be true to God. We are part of a community that belongs to Christ, and we honor God with our faithful obedience. The construction that takes place during this phase of development prepares us for the next.

Sacrifice

As we delve deeper into God's Word, we yield to the

1John 14:6

leading and direction of the Holy Spirit. Sometimes we give up things that were once precious to us in order to fulfill the purposes of God. The ministry of Christ and His church consume more and more of our time. We eagerly use our talents to serve Him through that with which He has equipped us. We invest our finances into the kingdom of God because we believe Christ and His church are the hope of the world. We willingly give time, talent, and treasure to Jesus Christ because we know through first-hand experience that it is greater to give than it is to receive. We now have ownership in the kingdom of God and launch into the final phase of development.

Declaration

At this point you are so excited about what God has done in your life that you begin declaring how God in His mercy brought you through the first three phases. You begin to communicate to people how you have tasted the truth of Christ and found it to be sweet. Jesus has changed you into a living part of His earthly temple by forgiving you and cleansing you from your sin. Your experience of that forgiveness is so awesome you now sacrifice to maximize the declaration of His mercy to the world. God now has you at a place in life where you are investing in people.

God develops you through the Holy Spirit so you can fulfill the great commandment.

> "Teacher, which is the greatest commandment in the Law?" Jesus replied: "'Love the Lord your God with all your heart and with all your soul and with all your mind.' This is the first and greatest commandment. And the second is like it: 'Love your neighbor as yourself.' All the

Law and the Prophets hang on these two commandments"(Matthew 22:36-40).

God's greatest desire is for you and me to show Him that we love Him by treating each other the way He treats us.

To accomplish this, He personally trains us as His children so we can understand how to treat others. He leads us through these four phases of spiritual development with firmness and consequences wrapped in grace, patience, mercy, and love, which is the picture of a divine shelter of development. From first-hand experience, we have all we need to construct a human shelter where our families receive the same treatment from us that we receive from God. Regardless of your circumstances, as you read these words, you have available to you that which is necessary to develop your family in Christ. A single mom raising your children alone, grandparents taking care of abandoned kids, or a step dad rearing a blended family, God has promised, "never will I leave you, never will I forsake you." Remember, it takes a warrior to develop a warrior.

Before you are able to begin the development of your family, it may be necessary for you to connect with God. Is He calling you to follow Him? Just bow your head and pray, "Jesus, I believe You are the way, the truth, and the life. Please forgive me of my sins, come into my life, and begin the process of my spiritual development in You, Amen." *"The name of the LORD is a strong tower; the righteous run to it and are safe"* (Proverbs 18:10). Once you run into the divine shelter, you are ready to transfer the values of God to your family.

Chapter 3

Marriage Is the Master's Model
Developing Deep Authentic Relationships

The Model

Marriage is not a human right; it is a divine institution! Marriage is a sacred union between one man and one woman, and it must be defined as such. If it is anything else, call it what you will, but do not call it a marriage. Any other arrangement is not made in heaven.

> *The LORD God said, "It is not good for the man to be alone. I will make a helper suitable for him." . . . Then the LORD God made a woman from the rib he had taken out of the man, and he brought her to the man. The man said, "This is now bone of my bones and flesh of my flesh; she shall be called 'woman, 'for she was taken out of man. For this reason a man will leave his father and mother and be united to his wife, and they will become one flesh* (Genesis 2:18, 22-24).

When a man and woman unite before God, He no longer views them as two, but one. Any attempt to redefine the definition of marriage is an attempt to redefine God's creation and the very moral fabric of society. Every pastor, politician, teacher, policeman, and person who loves people must be concerned with protecting the institution of marriage.

In this one-flesh union, God brings a man and woman together to share life fully and completely. This new relationship is elevated above all other relationships, even that of blood relatives. Inside the bond of marriage, nothing is to be withheld between two human beings. God ordained marriage to serve as the vehicle needed to model His character and values. Maintaining a marriage is hard work and will require the manifestation of God's character and values to remain strong and healthy. Children observe parents as they relate to one another, up close and personal. Behind the four walls of a home, children watch two souls interact with each other.

What You See Is What You Get

Ultimately an individual's identity is formed through one's experience with his or her family. Parents instill into their children their character and values by the lives they live and the relationships within the home. What you see inside of your home when no one but the family is present is the real deal. God designed the family to be a place of openness. Originally Adam and Eve were not ashamed of their nakedness. But after their disobedience to God, they sought to achieve the great cover up. Humans are experts at hiding things from each other. But our feeble attempts at hiding from one another can only last so long. Eventually, the fig leaves dry out, become brittle, break, and leave us in very awkward situations. Therefore, when we leave our homes we make sure we are wearing fresh fig leaves to keep our image in tact, but in the comfort and security of our homes we relax and let our guard down. This is what makes marriage such an incredible creation of God. It is the perfect place to develop relationships and model the principles in Deuteronomy 6. In the midst of this authenticity, values and character are caught, not taught. If Christian parents would get serious about authentically modeling God's values and character, our world would change.

It's a Shelter Not a Zoo

To say you are authentic is one thing; to be authentic is quite another. One of the greatest accomplishments we can achieve for our children is authenticity in our marriages. A lack of authenticity impacts character and value development in children more than we realize. We go through life ignoring obvious problems in our relationships because fear paralyzes us. We are afraid to deal with relational issues because we don't know what will happen when we do. So we allow these issues to become huge elephants and remain in our shelters, significantly hindering the relational development of our children because our shelters are not designed for them. A marriage should be the best model of authenticity on the planet.

Why is it so difficult to achieve authenticity in our relationships? When a man and a woman decide to become a family, it's not long before someone experiences emotional pain. Everyone at some time has experienced hurt because of the actions of someone else. The typical reaction to emotional pain is pride. Instead of dealing with the apparent elephant, we choose to soak in prideful pity, wondering how someone could be so thoughtless toward us. When we indulge in prideful pity then resentment toward the other person begins to build. Instead of going to a deeper level in the relationship by confronting the elephant and dealing with the pain, we tend to withdraw from the one we love. Understand that the elephant is not the action committed against us; rather it is the pain we feel because of the action. It is essential to understand this because when it comes time to confront the elephant you must be able to identify it. If you cannot, then you will only complain about what the person did instead of communicating how you feel.

This scenario happens over and over in any relationship that has depth. If we are going to achieve authenticity in our marriage, we must realize this is not about what our spouse did so much as it is about an elephant (an issue) trying to barge in and make himself at home in our relationships. There is not enough room in a shelter to allow elephants to occupy any space.

> *Therefore each of you must put off falsehood and speak truthfully to his neighbor, for we are all members of one body. "In your anger do not sin": Do not let the sun go down while you are still angry, and do not give the devil a foothold* (Ephesians 4:25-27).

The Bible teaches we are to put off falsehood and speak truthfully with each other. In my interpretation, this is a command to be authentic! According to this passage if we fail to be authentic we give the enemy a foothold in the relationship, preventing us to go deeper. So if I allow an elephant to come between the one I love and me, it impacts my entire family.

Kids need a good authentic model from which they can learn. By good model I am not referring to children observing their parents going to church, doing devotions, and praying together. Those things are all healthy and good, but they do not serve as a sufficient model for the character and values of Christ. Too often they become a form of self-righteousness and a stumbling block to our children. A good model is not structured and legalistic; rather a good model is dynamic and authentic. A good model creates opportunities for children to witness their parents in the midst of difficult struggles while manifesting the character and values of Christ. When they see the love of Christ modeled in the midst of a struggle, they see reason to follow Christ. Children recognize authenticity when they see it. The flip side of this coin is that children can also spot a fake the moment one enters a room. If Christ's followers would begin to approach their relationships with authenticity and speak the truth in love, we could reach the world for Christ by default simply because the world craves depth in relationships.

Dig Deep

When we dig deep into our relationships, we operate from a position of truth that is insurmountable for the enemy. There are three things that will take your relationships deeper.

Humility: You will have to make up your mind to swallow your pride and humble yourself before God and other people. You must be aware of and watch out for self-pity. Be conscious of the fact that just because you have become a Christ-follower you are not immune to pride causing you to harbor resentment toward someone. Resentment will create a wedge in a relationship. It takes humility to acknowledge this and humble yourself before God. But there is an incredible benefit when we live this way. James 4:10 says to *"humble yourselves before the Lord, and he will lift you up."* If you are willing to humble yourself and admit there is a problem in your relationship, God will operate in the midst of that humility and elevate the relationship above the problem.

Vulnerability: Once you are willing to be humble the next step is vulnerability. There is always risk involved when you are building relationships. When you put yourself out there, it can be frightening. To open up to a person and admit we have an issue that needs to be worked through can be terrifying. The reason for the feeling of terror is because you realize you are subject to being hurt. It all depends on the reaction of the other person. But if your relationships are going to go deeper, then you must overcome your fear and practice vulnerability.

Faith: It takes faith to delve below the surface in relationships. If you put yourself out there, you have to believe that God is going to be in the situation. You also have to believe in the other person. So what we are talking about here is being vulnerable enough to approach someone else about what he or she has done that is causing you emotional pain. The other person may or may not be aware that the situation even exists. Rather than allowing frustration and resentment to build until the other person in the relationship figures it out, practice humility, vulnerability, and faith; raise the awareness of the situation and take the relationship deeper. The "elephant" in our relationship must be run out of the shelter before it takes up all the space.

It is important to deal with how you feel not with what the person did. This has a disarming effect and makes the situation about "our" relationship and not about "your" actions. Your goal is to communicate the following: "We are in this together and I am concerned about our relationship going deeper. I want to raise your awareness that there is an elephant barging into our relationship and I want to kick him out before damage is done." When children see parents interacting at this depth, it will change their lives because they see a model of Christ-like character interacting before their very eyes. It is authentic and they know it. Is God going to be in the midst of the interaction between father and mother, husband and wife? Without a shadow of doubt I am convinced He will. This is how we are supposed to live.

If fathers and mothers do not interact with each other at this level I am certain the wickedness of the world will seize these relationships with a death grip. Our children will benefit greatly when we model this depth of interaction as husband and wife. You may be a single parent wondering how to model this type of behavior without a spouse. Conflict resolution based on feelings and not personalities should permeate all of your relationships. Marriage is not the only place children should see this kind of interaction, but God designed marriage to be the first place they see it. The good news is Jesus shows us how to interact with people at this level.

Following the Rabbi

Christ modeled this behavior for us in the thirteenth chapter of John's gospel. Jesus had been ministering for three years and He had personally mentored twelve guys. One was a tax collector, and others were fishermen by trade, guys He specifically chose. He called them out of a mundane existence and became their rabbi. These men witnessed Jesus change water into wine, raise the dead, heal the sick, cast out demons, and walk on water. Their lives were transformed because of their relationship with Him.

Arrangements had been made for them to have a secret dinner. It had to be secret because the chief priests and scribes were seeking to kill Jesus. So they met to have their Last Supper with Him. The Twelve would have worn sandals; this was a very arid climate so their feet would have been dry and uncomfortable. It was customary to wash the dust off your guests' feet when they entered your home. Normally the host delegated the menial task of washing feet to a servant; since the banquet was a secret no servants were available. None of the disciples volunteered for the menial task either; to do so would have been an admission of inferiority. Obviously, the disciples were well aware of the situation and all wanted their feet washed, but no one was willing to volunteer. Again there is an elephant in the room!

Now Jesus is fully God but He was also fully human. So what might have been going through His mind? Hebrews 4:15 teaches He has been tempted in every way we have so He may have thought something like this: *Who is going to wash my feet Don't these guys realize how much I have invested in them For three years I have personally mentored them. I have provided their meals and entrusted my power to them. They have first-hand experience of my miracles! Don't they realize I am God in the flesh? They are so selfish. This is the last night I have with them and I cannot believe they are treating me this way!* He might have entertained these thoughts, but actually Jesus chose to model authenticity.

Jesus humbled Himself, became vulnerable, exhibited faith in God the Father, and confronted the elephant in the room. By the world's standards everything screamed that these guys needed to be rebuked, but Jesus did the opposite. He chose instead to model to His disciples how to take relationships deeper, and it just blew His disciples away. With each one He poured water from the basin over their feet and washed the dust and discomfort away. By serving them in this manner, Jesus declared the confidence He had in them.

We can learn three invaluable truths from our Rabbi's model.

When we are authentic we experience the full extent of love. Jesus showed the Twelve the full extent of His love. When you are authentic with your spouse and children you experience and understand a deeper level of love.

Humility is not a human characteristic; it is spiritual. Even after seventeen years of ministry in the trenches, I still have to make myself engage in authentic, humble behavior. You must choose to exercise humility, vulnerability, and faith because it is a spiritual characteristic. That is why we say there is an elephant in the room because it is easier to ignore it than it is to confront it. Humility will never come naturally to you.

Serving each other is the key to deep relationships. When you are humble enough to serve others, the enemy has no place to operate within your relationships. This is what it means to follow Christ. If we practice authenticity in our marriages, our children will pick up on it and imitate it. They recognize your relationship has depth. Is your shelter a comfortable place exuding authenticity or do the elephants take up all the space, leaving little or no room for depth?

Chapter 4

Close Combat

Developing Rules of Engagement

Fighting Fair

Fighting is part of human nature. When we become Christians and join a local church, often we are told that followers of Christ do not engage in that kind of behavior. That is ridiculous! Christ's followers fight all the time; we just tell people we don't. So to be true to what we have learned lets just get it out there and admit that we fight, at different times and for different reasons. Arguing is a real part of who we are. Whenever you put several different personalities under one roof for an extended time, there will be conflict. I have heard Christians say that parents should never allow their kids to see them fight. I wholeheartedly disagree with that philosophy. Children need to observe their parents struggling with problems and dealing with conflict. Kids learn how to relate to other people by watching their parents relate to one another. This is the way God designed it to be. If parents are committed to developing their children for Christ, then marriage is the greatest place for their children to learn how to fight fair.

How to Fight Fair

What causes fights in the first place? An ideal person to look to for instruction in fighting fair is James, the half-brother of Jesus. I have three brothers and if James' experience was anything like mine he had to have had a squabble or two with Jesus while he was growing up. Can you imagine having to hold your own if Jesus was your brother? I don't know if James argued with Jesus, but I do know John 7:5 says that Jesus' brothers did not believe He was the Messiah, the Son of God.[1] That would probably lead to some heated conversations in this family. I can only speculate, but I do know for certain that James understood why we fight.

> *What causes fights and quarrels among you? Don't they come from your desires that battle within you?* (James 4:1).

Simply stated, we fight because we have competing desires. I want what I want and you want what you want. That may be why someone invented dual climate control for cars. I want it hot; you want it cold. Learn to work through these competing desires or they will destroy your relationships. Since competing desires are inevitable, how do we fight fair?

Make Peace With God

One reason you might have a lot of turmoil in your home is because you are not at peace with God. If you do not have peace with God, then you expect other people to meet the needs in your life that only God can meet. An unmet need in your life can cause you to be a very unpleasant person to be around. Now it's impossible to fight fair. You may have thought this book would give you the answers to the difficulties you face with raising

---

[1]After the resurrection of Jesus, James did believe.

your children, but you fail to realize your greatest obstacle is the battle you are in with God. If you are not at peace with God you cannot possibly be at peace with your spouse or children.

Maybe you have undergone spiritual transformation, yet you're still in a fight with God. He may be asking you to do something you don't want to do. A divine struggle impacts your relationships with people more than you realize. Every time you fight with God, it requires a certain amount of energy and concentration to block it out of your mind in order to function normally. You end up dealing with something you shouldn't have to deal with, which causes fatigue. Learning to listen and obey God makes getting along with other people easier, especially those who are closest to you. The greatest gift you could give your family may be laying this book aside and making peace with God before reading further.

If you are unwilling to make peace with God you are compromising the safety of your shelter. Failure to make peace with God makes it impossible to talk to Him about the problems you're having with other people. The most important relationship in your life is your relationship with God. How can God show you how to deal with someone else when you are not even willing to listen to how He wants you to deal with Him? Listen to what James says about this.

> *You want something but don't get it.*
> *You kill and covet, but you cannot have*
> *what you want. You quarrel and fight. You*
> *do not have, because you do not ask God*
> (James 4:2).

Our problems would work out if we would just talk to God about them. We need to learn to vent vertically and not horizontally. We don't have a problem telling people how we feel about them. However, amazing changes occur within ourselves when we learn to discuss our feelings about others with God. When I vent vertically to God it alleviates my need to vent horizontally with others. Usually this is the case because it is during these times God reveals some serious blunders in my own behavior. Generally people do just the opposite. They vent horizontally with others, and then invite God into the situation to clean it up. Families often get into huge fights and expect God to fix it. Try venting vertically so God can teach you how to fight fair.

Assume a Low Position

When you fight you want to be in an advantageous position. Think of the pictures of the wrestling team in a yearbook. The wrestler crouches with his hands forward ready to do battle. He is assuming a low position in order to counter an attack from his opponent. Basketball players are coached to position themselves for the triple threat. From this position a player can pass, dribble, or shoot. When it comes to fighting fair we can combine these two concepts and assume a low position that contains a triple threat.

James identifies the low position. *Humble yourselves before the Lord, and he will lift you up* (James 4:10). According to James we are to go down low so God can lift us up. The half-brother of Christ is showing us how to practice what we have learned from Jesus in the last chapter. But that is not typically what people do. People usually raise them selves up in order to get in the first shot, believing that if they get the first punch in they can win the fight. When people get their feelings hurt, the natural inclination is to rise up and make the situation about "self" in order to win the argument. People do not naturally think about the consequences of winning. You may win the argument by raising yourself up, but you might lose your child or spouse in the process. Once you assume the low position, winning is not as important as fighting fair.

The Triple Threat

1. *How much of this is my fault?*

A person must immediately ask how much of what is happening is my fault? How much am I contributing to what is happening here? That is not the natural human response, but then we are not talking about the natural man. We are talking about the supernatural response of the Holy Spirit who is living in us. We are talking about the fruit of the Spirit growing in our lives! Before accusing and attacking the other person, ask how much of the argument is your fault.

Ask yourself what you have done wrong in the situation before focusing on what the other person has done. Take a look at yourself first because there is no one-person problem in relationships. You cannot say that is "your problem," or "their problem"; rather, it is "our problem." If I am in the middle of it, then it is mine too. Therefore, I must assess how much of it is my fault. Am I being too demanding, unrealistic, oversensitive, impatient, or insensitive?

2. *Acknowledge strengths and weakness*

The next step is to acknowledge that everyone has strengths and weaknesses. Do you realize that God has wired you with a unique set of strengths? There are just some things you are naturally good at. You don't even have to work hard to accomplish them. Some people are naturally gifted communicators while others are horrible. It's not that they are wrong or don't know how to fight fair. Some people are incapable of saying what they are thinking in the heat of a battle. Your opponent is so quick on his or her feet that he or she nails you between the eyes before you can get anything out. Then before you say anything, you are nailed again. Afterwards you think of everything you should have said! That is a weakness and the person who has the strength of communication should realize he or she has that strength over you. In order for the communicator to assume a low position he or she must keep his or her mouth shut and help the other person communicate. If the communicator fails to do this, he is perverting the very gift God gave him. *Even a fool is thought wise if he keeps silent, and discerning if he holds his tongue* (Proverbs 17:28). A lot of Christ's followers look foolish because they cannot close their mouths in the middle of an argument. If I am a strong communicator talking to a person who does not have the strength of communication, I have a responsibility to hold back and let you talk while I listen. If I am a weak communicator I need to realize you can help me communicate better. A person who fights fair acknowledges strengths and weaknesses.

3. Talk to someone else about you

Go to someone you can trust to talk about you. When you are having relationship problems, seek a wise person who will listen and help you talk about your behavior. The majority of the time we call our friends and complain about others. "You're never going to believe what he did." That is not healthy at all. When it is time for counsel we need to find someone who will challenge us to focus on what part we played in the fight. I recommend you tell the person up front what you want from him or her. Ask your friend to listen and carefully scrutinize what you may have done wrong. Tell him or her you are not interested in comments on what the other person did. Your goal is to have a critical, unbiased, objective ear and mind focused on you.

For sake of illustration, let's say you have a teenage daughter with whom you plan to have a difficult father/daughter talk. On this particular occasion you are having a terrible time understanding her and she has a difficult time understanding you. The two of you are butting heads and you are confident she needs your help in correcting her course with this experience. Your conversation heats up and the two of you exchange words, which ends up in a fight that is not productive at all. The wise thing to do may be to take a break for a few minutes. Go to your wife and ask her how she thinks you are doing. Let her critique your words and tone and give you honest feedback. Listen to what she says. If she advises that you have been too tough, don't jump on her for giving you honest feedback! Remember, you should not feel attacked because she is there to help you build this shelter of safety. She is not against you and she is no help at all if she is not honest with you.

Help people talk about themselves, not about others. However, it requires courage to speak up and re-direct people when they begin sharing unproductive thoughts. When someone talks about others' behavior instead of focusing on his or her own, politely remind that person you can't help those others, only him or her. This immediately helps the person assume the healthy place of the low position. If both parties can assume the low position, then harmony is achieved.

Work It Out

Finally, in order to fight fair we must be compelled to work it out.

"In your anger do not sin: Do not let the sun go down while you are still angry" (Ephesians 4:26).

To protect your shelter, establish the rule that conflicts must be worked through before going to bed. Abby and I have a standing rule in our marriage. If we are angry about anything, we must make the other one aware and work it out before we go to sleep. You can go to sleep with an issue unresolved but never go to sleep angry. I learned this lesson early in my marriage.

One evening Abby and I went to bed and I was still angry about something. I got in bed and didn't say a word. I tossed, turned, flopped, beat my pillow, and sighed in utter disgust several times. I got out of bed and went to the kitchen where I proceeded to bang dishes and cabinet doors while getting something to drink. I returned to bed with as much movement and noise as possible. I lay there, getting more and more worked up. My heart rate increased and my teeth were clenched. Abby lay next to me, sleeping like a baby! Finally I gave in to Ephesians 4:26, woke her up, and told her I was angry and we had to work it out. I just told her my heart was not where it needed to be and I had to get rid of the anger. We talked for awhile, worked it out, and slept in each other's arms.

I could have chosen not to wake her up, but I would have been guilty of jeopardizing the health of my relationship with her. The relationship would have been at risk because chances are good I would have let it go and forgot about it. But each time we let deep hurt go unresolved, our hearts are at risk of becoming harder toward the ones we love. The harder your heart gets toward someone the easier it is to push him or her away, leading to increased conflict. One day you wake up finding it difficult to recognize the value of the one you used to love. This all happens because people let the sun go down on their anger. Your kids are watching; fight fair and work it out.

Chapter 5

Raising Little Warriors

Developing Your Kids the Way God Develops You

What is the best approach to developing children? How do we decide? Teachers, doctors, counselors, ministers, our parents, and, of course, Oprah all attempt to influence the way we raise our children. With all of these competing voices vying for our attention, how do we filter the noise and make the right decisions about parenting? Raising children and filtering the noise is really not complicated. The secret is simply to develop our children the way God develops us and we will be successful parents.

When we choose to follow Christ, God develops us beneath the protection of a divine shelter. *The name of the LORD is a strong tower; the righteous run to it and are safe* (Proverbs 18:10). Deuteronomy six teaches we are to love God with all our heart, mind, and strength. Jesus verified the significance of this truth:,

> *Teacher, which is the greatest commandment in the Law?" Jesus replied: "'Love the Lord your God with all your heart and with all your soul and with all*

your mind.' This is the first and greatest commandment. And the second is like it: 'Love your neighbor as yourself.' All the Law and the Prophets hang on these two commandments (Matthew 22:36-40).

Everything is secondary to these two commandments. The first commandment describes our relationship to God. God develops us beneath His divine shelter where we experience His grace and truth. The second commandment implies that people should experience grace and truth from Christ's followers as a result of their experience with God. What better place to begin than with the family? Our children should develop beneath the protection of a human family shelter where they also experience grace and truth from their parents. We are to love our kids the way we love ourselves by treating them the way God treats us.

My experience with the Lord has convinced me He has raised me up as a warrior in His Kingdom. Everyday I live is an opportunity to love God with all my being and to love my neighbor as myself. God uses me to overcome evil with good. It can be very motivational to see yourself as a warrior in the midst of a battle that is being waged against evil. It gives meaning to my life and makes me aware that all of my decisions and actions make a difference in this world. God treats us as His warriors and the Apostle Paul agrees.[1] Therefore, I have taught my children from the time they could speak that they are little warriors and princess warriors for Jesus Christ. One day each of them must accept the atoning sacrifice of Christ on the cross. I am not just teaching them about a future decision they will make; I am teaching them to follow Christ. I impress this lifestyle on their hearts by developing them the way God develops me. Ask any of

---

[1] 2 Timothy 2:3

my children what they are and they will tell you they are a warrior or warrior princess for Jesus. Let's look at four areas of warrior development.

Understand Your Warrior

To treat my kids the way God treats me I must understand them.

> *As a father has compassion on his children, so the LORD has compassion on those who fear him; for he knows how we are formed, he remembers that we are dust* (Psalm 103:13-14).

God knows what makes us tick and He understands how we are wired. One day while speaking at a junior high school I asked the students, "If you could give your parents one piece of advice and you knew they would listen what would you say?" Without hesitation one young man exclaimed, "Try to understand me!" This is a major complaint teenagers have about their parents. Obviously, a generational divide exists but this does not excuse parents from working hard at understanding their children. Parents, we must study our kids and seek to understand them.[2]

Train a child in the way he should go, and when he is old he will not turn from it (Proverbs 22:6). is probably one of the most misquoted and misunderstood verses in the Bible. Many people believe this Scripture means that if they raise their kids in church and teach them to make a decision for Christ, they will hold onto it all their lives. Their children may stray from the faith but if they have laid the right foundation, sooner or later their children will return as the prodigal son does in the gospel of Luke. I have heard it preached this way from the pulpit and I have listened to parents claim it as a

---

[2]Proverbs 24:3

promise. But that is not what this verse teaches.

The key to understanding this verse is the phrase *way he should go*. It is not to be interpreted the way *you want* him to go; rather, it is the way *he should* go. Many parents make the destructive mistake of trying to relive their lives through their children. It is not uncommon to see a parent that excelled in a particular activity when he or she was young make their kids participate in the same activity, even when their children are not interested. Another tragic mistake parents of more that one child make is comparison to siblings. At times a parent will say, "Why can't you be more like your brother? He does great in school and makes excellent grades. You are always in trouble. Can you please be more like your brother?" The answer to that question is NO! One child cannot be like the other child because they are two entirely different people. I have five children and they are as different as night and day, hot and cold. God uniquely designed each of their personalities and you cannot develop them the same way. One will be bent in this direction while the other will have a tendency to go in the opposite direction. The job of a parent is to understand how God has wired each child. That is how God develops us. There are billions of people on the planet right now and no two people have the same fingerprints. God created you with a unique personality and He relates to you and loves you with that personality. Part of warrior development is working very hard at understanding your children the way God understands you.

Accepting Your Warrior

Understanding your warriors enables you to accept them just the way God uniquely designed them. Some children are a challenge to develop and instead of acceptance they often experience rejection from their parents. You may think I don't understand your situation because you have a strong-willed child, but I do for I too have a strong-willed child. Some children will do as they are told, making you look as if you are a parenting genius. Then there are the children who make messes, break things, and get into trouble all the time! They can make us look like we are too irresponsible to be parents. Do not let negative thoughts influence your understanding of your warriors. It is easy for parents to think something is wrong with a child who is harder to deal with compared to his or her siblings. If you are in this situation I want to encourage you. What you really possess in your family is a gift from God. If you have a child that is always exploring and challenging things, then chances are God has placed a soul under your authority that is wired for leadership. Don't compare that child with a brother or sister because comparison will damage their self-esteem and cloud your perception of him or her. Often these scenarios within a family result in rebellion. Decide to accept your children just the way they are, developing them within their uniqueness. You have a potential leader of the next generation that must be developed the way God wired them. That is called grace and is the way God develops you.

God does not ask us to get our acts together before He begins developing us. God urges us to come underneath the protection of His divine shelter just the way we are. If you are going to treat your children the way God treats you then you must give them the opportunity to develop underneath the protection of your human shelter. Have you made the effort to study and understand your children so you can accept them just the way they are? If you fail to accept your kids for who they are, I must warn you of a potential storm that is threatening your family.

At the age of twelve or thirteen your children will enter early adolescence. At this stage of life they will naturally develop independence. If you have not accepted them the way they are designed and have attempted to make them into something else, your children will become very effective at wearing masks. They will come home from school and before they walk in the door they will put on a mask that pleases you. They will pretend to be something they are not in order to gain your acceptance and keep you off their back. The very shelter that is designed to be a place of vulnerable authenticity will become a masquerade. What you see will be what you want to see, but it will not be who your child is. If this takes place then your children will resent you for the rest of their lives, and rightly so, because they could not be who they really were in the very shelter in which God placed them.

One of the reasons I have such a great relationship with my parents today is because I was able to be myself growing up in the shelter they provided for me. My brothers and I were all unique and different and our parents allowed us to be ourselves, developing us within those traits. The more children involved, the more challenging this becomes because you must be fair and distinct simultaneously. Being fair as well as distinct requires creativity because your children will not all respond to the same treatment. Have you intentionally accepted all of your children as gifts from God? I would encourage you to do so; you will become more effective with the third area of warrior development.

Disciplining Your Warrior

The writer of Hebrews says, *The Lord disciplines those whom He loves* (12:6). What could be more plain or simple? God disciplines us. If you are a follower of

Christ living contrary to God's Word, expect a divine spanking. If you are a child of God and you fail to support the growth of His Kingdom by giving the first ten percent of your income to the local church, you can expect to be disciplined by God. If a follower of Christ dates people who are not committed to His Kingdom, God will discipline you. From first-hand experience God's discipline is not a pleasant experience. But I am thankful for God's discipline because in the midst of that uncomfortable feeling I am developed. What a demonstration of God's love for me.

Now, it is important to clarify that I do not believe God causes people to get cancer or die because they disobey Him. There are those who would teach such, but I am not in that camp. I believe sickness and death are the result of a fallen world, which will remain in that condition until Christ returns to the earth. When I talk about the discipline of the Lord I am referring to conviction that leads to anxiety and stymies our growth as Christians. When our spiritual growth is hampered, we are not in a state of production. If I am not producing spiritual fruit in my life, then I am not fulfilling the purpose for which I was created. This puts me in a state of disharmony with God and keeps me from enjoying life. It is a very unpleasant place to be and I believe that is how God disciplines us through the presence of the Holy Spirit. If God disciplines us then it logically follows that we should discipline our children. The Bible says if I do not discipline my kids then two things are true about me. First, failure to discipline my kids proves I really don't love them. Proverbs 13:24 teaches: *He who spares the rod hates his son, but he who loves him is careful to discipline him.* Second, failure to discipline shows I'm participating in their destruction. Listen to what Proverbs 19:18 (Good News) says: *Discipline your children while they are young enough to learn.*

If you don't you're helping them destroy themselves.
How should you discipline your warriors? Here are
three disciplinary principles I follow while training my
warriors.

1. Discipline calmly. Never discipline out of anger or
   frustration. If you are angry or frustrated then *you*
   need a time out.

2. Discipline quickly. Never delay it. Don't use, "Wait
   until your father gets home!" or "Wait until we get
   home. Small children do not have that frame of
   reference. If one of my children unbuckles his or her
   seatbelt I find a safe place to pull over and execute
   discipline quickly.

3. Discipline sparingly. Don't do it all the time. You get
   more effect if you are strategic in your decision of
   when to execute discipline.

Control your child now while he or she is young, or
when your child is older that lack of control can lead to
the destruction of his or her life. You may be a single
mom with a strong-willed child and thinking, "How can
I do this?" Your power source is the Holy Spirit. Ask
Him to help you get control of your child just like He
helps Christ get control of you!

The Apostle Paul admonishes, *Fathers, do not
embitter your children, or they will become discouraged*
(Colossians 3:21). Make sure you do not discipline kids
for being kids. You discipline them for rebellion and
there is a big difference between the two. One day I had
been working on a fifth wheel trailer I had bought for
our family to camp in. I was packing the wheel bearings
so I had the tires off. Since I had the tires off I decided
to paint the frame. Several hours later I was putting
it back together and Joel comes out and says, "Dad,
you should come in the shop and look at what Jonah
is doing." That was bad news because Joel had been

trained to always notify mom and dad when Jonah and Faith start getting creative. So I asked Joel, "What's he doing?" to which he responded with his finger on his chin, "Well, lets just say he's painting his tool box." I found Jonah and Faith with black spray paint all over them and his nice orange toolbox. Paint was all over my cabinets and on the shop floor. Jonah looked up with a smile loaded with pride and said, "Look daddy!" I was angry because he had made a mess and used all my paint. But I paused and thought about what had happened and why. I did not spank him because it was my fault this had happened. I knew when I put that paint down on the ground I should have put it out of reach because if Jonah saw it he could not resist. We should never discipline our children for being kids, which brings us to our final area of warrior development.

Love Your Warrior

Loving your warrior will do more for his or her confidence and security than anything else you can do. Your warrior needs affection; physical contact, with hugs, kisses, and pats on the back. Even if they are thirteen years old, pull them up in your arms and hug them. They may resist and act like they hate it, but make them deal with the misery because deep down it means the world to them.

Your warrior needs affirmation. We shape them with the words we speak over them. Parents want to build up their children and encourage them. Sometimes when my children are focused on something I will interrupt them and say, "Hey Joel . . . Joel!" "What dad?" "Do you know how much I love you?" "This much?" "No, more than that! Do you know why I love you?" "Because I cleaned my room?" "Nope." "Why dad?" "Because you're my son. That's why Joel!" I do this intentionally with all my kids because I want them to know they are loved with an unconditional love.

Your warrior needs attention, the number one way kids sense they are loved. You must allow them to interrupt you and show you things. What is important to them must be important to you. Take time out to play a game or read a book. A lot of people want to believe that quality time is more important than quantity. I think our children would disagree and tell us that quantity is more important to them than quality. God has looked down from His throne and placed a warrior or princess warrior under your care. He has given you the task of developing a warrior to impact the world for Him. As you develop your little warrior make sure you treat him or her the way God treats you.

Chapter 6

Controlling Your Warrior

Developing Your Shelter's System of Quality Control

Parental Control

I will never forget the day Abby and I brought our firstborn, Joel, home from the hospital. It was such a thrilling experience for us to be parents. We pulled in the garage, took Joel in the house, unbuckled him from his car seat, and laid him in his crib. The two of us stood over his crib looking at this tiny human being. Standing there is when I realized we were on our own. There would be no nurse to come in and help us. No one was going to tell us what to do or when to do it. This was our son and we were in total control of him. I could not believe it was actually legal for us to bring him home because we had absolutely no idea what we were doing. Neither of us had any parenting experience, yet we had total control of this human being. He totally depended on us to meet every need of his life and we gladly sacrificed to meet his needs.

When God gives you or me children to take care of and nurture for Him, those children are totally under parental control. We feed them, dress them, bathe them, brush their teeth, and change their diapers; we do everything for them. Before we had children of our own, the snotty noses and smelly diapers of other children were really a problem for us. But when we became parents we wiped snot and changed diapers without a second thought. We do this because we have been transformed by the miracle of childbirth. We are amazed that this little person was actually created from our flesh and we are infatuated with meeting our child's needs. While this infatuation is healthy and normal, if not understood, it can be the very thing that causes children to fail during adolescence. Just as the Holy Spirit leads us through phases of spiritual development, God expects us to lead our children through phases of family development. You must overcome the infatuation of parental control.

Self-Control

From the day we bring them home we must intentionally find areas to move them from parental control to self-control. Some areas are easier to relinquish parental control of than others. For instance, when children are infants we put bibs on them, put food on their high chair tray and let them have at it. When they are finished we get a cloth and clean them up. However, when they get a little older we teach them a lesson in self-control by showing them how to use a fork and a napkin. Now when it comes to a three year old using a napkin to wipe his or her face, it is probably easier to do it ourselves, This is where I believe parents make a crucial mistake in the development of their children. Just because something is easier does not necessarily mean it is better. Parents must make a conscious effort to release parental control at every opportunity so their children can develop self-control in as many areas as possible as early as possible. By the time children reach early adolescence they need to have developed a solid, healthy ability to control themselves. You would be amazed at how well your children can comprehend these concepts if you will just make it a part of your day-to-day interaction. My children understand quite well the difference between parental control and self-control. If one of them is acting out I simply ask, "Do you want me to bring you under parental control?" The reply is always an emphatic no! To which I respond, "You better use self-control or I will execute parental control!" My children understand the advantage of self-control.

To assist you in the development of your children and their ability to comprehend parental and self-control, I would like to suggest a couple of strategies that have been helpful to me. The first is "The Reminder." I am a firm believer in spanking and spanking early in order to help children understand authority (Parental Control).

The Bible teaches us there is value in spanking. *Do not withhold discipline from a child; if you punish him with the rod, he will not die* (Proverbs 23:13). James Dobson says spanking should begin no sooner than 18 months and not happen after 12 years of age.[1] The more effective we are at administering this type of discipline the less often we have to implement it. Spanking children is hard work and a parent should be committed to the complete process before spanking a child. There are two things I believe parents should avoid at all costs before spanking their children. The first one is anger. I never spank my children when I am angry because spanking is about instruction and development, not anger and emotions. This is crucial because my children must understand that these consequences are a result of their behavior, not my emotions, and they know the

---

[1]Dobson, James C; *The New Dare to Discipline*, Tyndale House Publishers, (1970), Page 65.

difference. The second is to be sure you do not spank too hard. It should be just hard enough to bring tears and discomfort and not any harder. If you cannot control yourself in these two areas, you should not spank your children!

Once you administer a spanking you must follow it with instruction to complete the process. I always hold my children after they are spanked and I explain to them that I spanked them because they are under my control and I am trying to teach them how to have self-control and make good decisions. I tell them that I love them and I hold them until they are calm and able to tell me that they love me as well. My children have never experienced a spanking from me where they did not experience this love and instruction along with it. They have Dr. James Dobson to thank for that and he describes it best in his book *The New Dare to Discipline*, which is a must read for every parent.

> After emotional ventilation, the child will often want to crumple to the breast of his parent, and he should be welcomed with open, warm, loving arms. At that moment you can talk heart to heart. You can tell him how much you love him, and how important he is to you. You can explain why he was disciplined and how he can avoid the difficulty next time. This kind of communication is often impossible with other disciplinary measures . . . such as standing the youngster in the corner or taking away his favorite toy. A resentful child usually does not want to talk.[2]

In our home to help our kids comprehend parental control and consequences, we use the "reminder." It is a piece of plywood an eighth inch thick that is three inches wide and twelve inches long. My kids helped

---

[2]*The New Dare To Discipline*, 35.

me write the word *reminder* on it with a permanent marker. I asked them why they thought we wrote the word *reminder* on it. Jonah was three at the time and he immediately replied, "Because it reminds us of what we are supposed to do!" My children are motivated to exercise self-control because they know that parental control will be used to "REMIND" them of the consequences of their disobedience.

Another strategy I have implemented to help my children develop self-control at an early age is what I call "BREATHE." I use this technique more than anything else. It is not uncommon for my oldest daughter Faith to come running into the room, sobbing while at the same time exclaiming, "Brudders won't, (cry, cry) Jonah push me, (cry, cry,)." I have no idea what she is saying because she is emotionally out of control. Instead of giving into the temptation to rescue her and make it all go away, I take advantage of the opportunity and teach Faith a lesson in self-control. I look at her in the eyes and say, "Sugar Bear, BREATHE!" Now picture a three year old little girl with long, sandy blonde hair, big, blue, tear-filled eyes, taking a huge breath, with cheeks inflated to capacity, then exhaling and repeating the process several times until she regains her composure. This is what I mean when I say BREATHE!

I use the same tactic if one of my children is scared because they fell off the swing set or some other accident has taken place. I quickly assess each situation to determine if my child is hurt, scared, or just angry. If they are hurt I immediately go into rescue mode and bring them comfort. If they are scared or angry, then I go into teaching mode and engage in development. This is my job as a parent to give my children what is best for them in each situation. This is exactly how God treats us! Sometimes the Holy Spirit brings us comfort, at other times development. But we can be certain we always receive consistency. Are small children able to grasp this? Mine do!

One afternoon while I was preparing a sermon about raising children my cell phone rang. I answered and the caller said, "Mr. Holbrook, this is Mrs. Talley and I am having some trouble out of Jonah today. I placed a coloring sheet on his table and he scribbled all over it. I told him that we do not color like that in preschool and placed a new coloring sheet in front of him. He then proceeded to scribble all over the table. I tried to talk to him but he started pouting and he won't listen to anything I say. I have never experienced this with him before and I wanted to talk to you about it." I responded by letting her know that Jonah does have a temper and she is experiencing something we, too, have experienced with him. Jonah is very strong willed and when he turns his mouth south he is very difficult to deal with. Sometimes I have to pull him aside and get him to think about his behavior and the consequences of it.

For instance one time Jonah was on his way home with his mother, his brother, and sisters. Jonah was angry because Joel ate all of his candy. I was outside when they arrived and he was fuming. Abby told me that he had cried all the way home. I asked him to talk with me and we sat down in the grass. He was so upset he could not explain what had happened so I said, "Jonah, BREATHE!" Once he calmed down I proceeded to tell him that this is not how you negotiate in life. I said, "Jonah don't you realize I have the ability to go to the store right now and buy you a case of candy?" Jonah's response, "What's negotiate?" I proceeded to teach him a very valuable life lesson and help him learn how to control himself.

I shared this story with his teacher and told her that I would talk to Jonah about the incident that took place at school. I suggested that she try this tactic if it happens again. I also informed her that if he does not cooperate that she need only to call me and I would drop what I was doing and come to the school and deal with it myself. One week later I received another call. "Mr. Holbrook, this is Mrs. Talley and I am having trouble with Jonah again. He took his scissors and cut up all of his paper. I said, "Jonah we don't do that with our scissors." He then proceeded to cut a chunk of his hair out. Mr. Holbrook, I cannot get him to do anything." I told Mrs. Talley that I would be there within the hour. I hung up the phone and went to the school. My plan was to check in at the office and spank Jonah with the principal present. But after meeting with Jonah's principal, he and I agreed to see how Jonah reacted to having to go to the principal's office.

So I sat in the main office awaiting Jonah's arrival. He had no idea I was at the school. When he rounded the corner and saw me, he fell apart. Crying uncontrollably Jonah said, "Daddy, I don't want to go to the principal's office. I am sorry daddy, I'm sorry!" To which I responded, "BREATHE, son BREATHE!" He finally regained his composure and said, "Daddy, I don't want to go see the principal." I said, "Jonah, you don't have a choice; this is your lack of self-control that has put you in this position. I will go in with you, but you will have to go in and negotiate with the principal yourself."

After a few minutes passed the principal opened his door and said, "Jonah, would you and your dad come in so we can visit about what happened in class today?" Jonah once again fell apart and started crying uncontrollably as he sat down in the chair in front of Mr. Parker's desk. I intentionally never said a word and keep in mind that Jonah was only four. As Mr. Parker started to talk to him, guess what Jonah started to do—

BREATHE! It was totally unprompted by me. All my intentional development was rewarded that day as I witnessed my son exercise self-control. It was all I could do to keep myself from bursting into tears because I was so proud of my boy. He had learned an important lesson in self-control and that is vital. The earlier I can get him to self-control the easier it is to get him under God's control.

God's Control

The more effective we are at teaching our children self-control, the easier it is for them to place themselves under God's control. I thank God my parents spanked me because I believe it made it easier for me to connect with God and respect Him as the ultimate authority in my life. I have never had a problem submitting to authority in any situation I have been in. I haven't always made the greatest choices but I have always respected authority. The reason I have not had a problem respecting authority is because my parents taught me from an early age that if I did not exhibit self-control they would enforce parental control. It didn't matter if it was an adult, a teacher, the preacher, a policeman, or a boss I found myself in trouble with. My mom and dad backed the authority figure in my life every time. There was never a question in my life whose side they would be on if I got into trouble. This is by far the greatest lesson my parents transferred to me.

This was an integral part of my development because when it came time for me to surrender my will to Christ it came easily for me. Now the Holy Spirit and the Word of God are the ultimate authority in my life. Because my parents instilled a respect for authority, I understand the necessity of submitting to God's control. This developmental process is crucial to instill in our children because this is exactly how God treats us. Remember the key to successful parenting is developing your children the way God develops you. Listen to the Apostle Peter's instructions about spiritual development:

> For this very reason, make every effort to add to your faith goodness; and to goodness, knowledge; and to knowledge, <u>self-control; and to self-control</u>, perseverance; and to perseverance, godliness; and to godliness, brotherly kindness; and to brotherly kindness, love. For if you possess these qualities in increasing measure, they will keep you from being ineffective and unproductive in your knowledge of our Lord Jesus Christ (2 Peter 1:5-8), [emphasis added].

According to Peter self-control is essential in making one productive and effective in their knowledge of Christ. The implication is obvious; the better I am at controlling myself, the easier it is to respect authority. The better I am at respecting authority, the easier it is to place myself under God's control. We do our children a serious disservice if we do not teach them self-control and respect for authority. By letting them get away with little things when they are young, we make it harder for them to connect with God when they are older. If our children fail to connect with God, they miss God's objective, the very purpose for which they were created. Scripture clearly teaches God's objective is *to bring all things in heaven and on earth together under one head, even Christ* (Ephesians 1:10). The objective of God is to bring everything under the head or control of Christ. If a life is lived outside of God's objective it is a life that is out of control and that is a dangerous place to be.

Out of Control

What happens when people lose control and have no respect for authority? In a word, CHAOS! We have witnessed it in professional sports with multimillion-dollar athletes choking coaches and spitting in the faces of umpires. We see it in Hollywood where Jerry Springer and Maury Povich run up television ratings by enticing people to lose control, then glorifying that loss of control with applause. One of the most shocking scenes took place when 35,000 people sought protection from the most destructive hurricane ever to strike the U.S. August 29, 2005 at 7:10 a.m. Hurricane Katrina made landfall. Many of the citizens of New Orleans did not heed the warnings and evacuate. They were told to seek safety in a makeshift shelter—The New Orleans Superdome. CNN described scenes of lawlessness and despair. There were reports of gun-totting teenagers, girls being raped, and military helicopters unable to bring supplies due to gunfire.[3] "We have suspended operations until they gain control of the Superdome," said Richard Zeuschlag, head of Acadian Ambulance, which was handling the evacuation of sick and injured people from the building."[4]

Call it a shelter if you want, but if there is no one maintaining and enforcing control of the group and the individuals, there is nothing safe about it. It is chaotic and it leads to destructive behavior. Your family is no different. It was designed by God to be a shelter of development. But if you do not maintain control, it will become a place of chaos and destruction. God moves you through phases of spiritual development and so you must help your children move from parental control to self-control, thereby making it easier for them to surrender to God's control. In the quote above, the ambulance responder said operations were suspended

---

[3]http://www.cnn.com/2005/WEATHER/09/01/katrina.impact/index.html.
[4]http://www.foxnews.com/story/0,2933,168112,00.html.

until they gained control of The Superdome. Think of the absurdity of that statement. They could not rescue people because no one was in control. This causes me to ask, "How could people act that way?" The answer to the question is quite simple. No one was prepared for the storm. If they had understood the magnitude of the storm, the government officials would have been prepared and had the situation under control from day one. Honestly, it is easier for me to comprehend the chaos and lack of control inside the Superdome than it is for me to understand the lack of control inside of families. There are too many people who are not prepared. If you do not have parental control, your children cannot learn self-control, therefore, it makes it very difficult to lead them to God's control. It is impossible to transfer the values of God if there is no control. You must be prepared to gain parental control and develop self-control from day one. It's all about control!

Chapter 7

Developing Your Warriors Worldview
Helping Kids Recognize and Embrace Truth

Bursting of the Bubble

There was a time in world history when everyone embraced the geocentric model. The sun comes up in the morning and goes down in the evening and appears to orbit the earth. But along came Copernicus who proposed that the earth actually orbited the sun. Copernicus gave us the heliocentric model and he was indeed correct. History teaches us that the dominant worldview at that time was indeed false. A worldview is simply the lens through which a person perceives the world and interacts with it.

A person's set of beliefs operates as a lens through which he or she makes decisions and live his or her life. Because you are reading this book, odds are good that you view the world and interact with it through the lens of Christianity. Seven major worldviews compete for our attention. While this is not the time to unpack each one, I believe this is the most important chapter in this book.

If you do not have a firm grasp of what you believe and why you believe it, you may end up with a hodgepodge worldview; a view in which you take a little of this and a little of that, not realizing it is contradicting the very faith you claim to believe. This is one of the most relevant issues the church has to address in our time.

It is no longer enough to know what you believe but you must also know why you believe what you believe. There was a time when society reinforced the Christian worldview. America had a Christian culture that served as a bubble of protection. Christianity was the dominant worldview and it influenced everything. Government, education, the arts, etc. were shaped within the context of a Christian worldview.

Television is a great example of this. While I was growing up in the seventies two of the most popular shows aired during primetime were "The Waltons" and "Little House on the Prairie." It was not uncommon to catch an episode of these shows that contained scenes at church and family prayer during meal times. The mainstream media reinforced Christian principles. But, the bubble has burst and those days are over. Now the dominant worldview reinforced by the mainstream media is moral relativism. If it feels good do it! Premarital sex, adultery, and homosexuality are glamorized nightly on all the major networks. Generally, if a character is a Christian he or she is portrayed as a hypocritical goof and ridiculed.

We are living and raising children in an environment inundated with information. Websites, commercials, sitcoms, The Discovery Channel, MTV, books, movies, and music are all available at your fingertips. It is impossible to keep children from experiencing this barrage of information. To buy music, just click a button with your mouse and you are listening within seconds. You and your family must process all of this information, which becomes more and more influential. Failure to understand your own worldview and that of others puts a person in danger of picking up bits and pieces of contradiction and formulating a hodgepodge worldview.

Spiritual Schizophrenia

You cannot take from two different worldviews and live a consistent life. You will end up being a spiritual schizophrenic. Christianity faces this major problem today. People hear something that sounds good and feels good, so they conclude that it must be right. Once this conclusion is drawn, they attach it to their theology without testing its validity. That is why there are so many people who claim to be followers of Christ, yet their lifestyles do not match their belief system. People try to harmonize competing worldviews and that just won't happen.

Unfortunately, many people have bought into the lie that taking their kids to church is what it means to be a Christian family. Nothing could be further from the truth. It is not enough to talk about God once or twice a week in church. God commanded your family to function as the primary vehicle that transfers His values to the next generation.

> *These commandments that I give you today are to be upon your hearts. Impress them on your children. Talk about them when you sit at home and when you walk along the road, when you lie down and when you get up. Tie them as symbols on your hands and bind them on your foreheads. Write them on the doorframes of your houses and on your gates* (Deuteronomy 6:6-9).

God expects daily life in the family to orbit around His identity, values, character, and relation to people. We are commanded to talk about Him when we get up, when we lie down, and when we walk or go about our daily activities. The NIV says we are to impress them on our children; the KJV says to teach them diligently. Both of these ideas are translated from the Hebrew word *shanan*, which means to whet or sharpen.

I remember, as a child, watching my dad sharpen his knife with a whetstone while watching a ball game on television. He oiled the stone and intentionally whet the blade back and forth with patience, balance, and precision until a razor sharp edge was achieved. If a knife is not held at the proper angle then the process has an adverse effect on the blade and dulls it. If a knife is whetted too much, then the edge becomes brittle and is subject to breaks. This is the idea Moses is conveying to parents. With patience, balance, and precision, intentionally whet your child against the Rock, until a keen edge is achieved. The psalmist asks, *For who is God besides the LORD? And who is the Rock except our God?* (Psalm 18:31).

Moses is speaking to the Israelites about taking possession of the Promised Land and he offers a challenge. Don't leave God out of your family's daily experience as you fulfill your destiny. This challenge applies to us as well. God wants to be the center of our family's daily experience. Why? Because it is certain our children will discover their identity, values, character, and relationships from within their family. Good or bad people do not leave home without these four things. Therefore God designed the family to be the place that centers all of life on Him.

When family life is in orbit around God, then development takes place with truth at the center. Truth is essential for healthy development. That is precisely why God commanded that He be the center of attention in family life. Often parents wonder why their children stray from the Christian faith when they enter late adolescence. I believe in many cases it is because they have not been equipped with a Christian worldview. How can we expect kids to embrace a faith that seems to be irrelevant to their everyday life experiences? If the only time children have discussions about God is on the trip to and from church orbiting around a sermon, then they are incapable of thinking "Christianly."

We live in a society that is inundated with moral relativism. This worldview teaches that moral absolutes do not exist, so if it feels good, do it. Each person determines what is right or wrong according to his or her own life experiences. Many kids that are raised in Christian homes can identify with Pilate when he asked Jesus, "What is truth?"[1] That is the most important question in life and we must equip our kids with the ability to embrace Christ's answer to Thomas when he asked Jesus, "How can we know the way?" Jesus answered, "I am the way and the truth and the life."[2] This is the reason God visited our world wrapped in the flesh of Jesus Christ. *"You are right in saying I am a king. In fact, for this reason I was born, and for this I came into the world, to testify to the truth. Everyone on the side of truth listens to me."*[3] The problem is not that we do not have the truth; the problem is we are not embracing the truth with the kind of passion that allows it to impact our behavior. We are failing to teach our children to view all life experiences through the lens of Christianity.

The Barna Group conducted a survey titled *Teenagers' Beliefs Moving Farther From Biblical Perspectives*. The survey concluded that while most of

---

[1]John 18:38
[2]John 14:5-6
[3]John 18:37

the teenagers surveyed claimed to be Christians, they clearly did not understand the Christian worldview. While Christian students have good intentions, their spiritual confusion leads to destructive decisions. The poll also pointed out that the dominant influences for young people are their parents and popular culture.[4] You can rest assured popular culture is influencing your kids with moral relativism. Your job is to help them recognize it!

Spiritual Geocentrism

We cannot pass our faith on to the next generation as merely a religion we associate with. Rather, we must pass it on as a worldview we perceive as true. Too often Christians are guilty of treating Christianity as a sidebar to their existence rather than the center of their being. The Christian worldview should impact your lifestyle. When Christ saves you from sin and you believe He is the Way, the Truth, and the Life, your entire view of the world is supposed to shift. Christ rearranges your life and you begin behaving differently as you obey the teachings of the Bible. But this is not the case among many followers of Christ. Too many Christ followers are geocentric with their faith. Instead of orbiting around God, they expect God to orbit around them. "God, here are my experiences; would You come and orbit around my life?"

Christianity is not geocentric; God designed it to be heliocentric. The reason kids who have been brought up in Christian homes struggle with their faith and lifestyle harmonizing is because parents are embracing spiritual geocentrism in a heliocentric world. The Son does not revolve around the world; the world revolves around the Son!

---

[4]http://www.barna.org/FlexPage.aspx?Page=BarnaUpdate&BarnaUpdateID=74

If you want to be successful at transferring the values of God to your children, then make sure you have a heliocentric faith. Every decision you make, activity you participate in, and relationship you develop should orbit around God. He has provided His Holy Spirit and the Bible to serve as the gravitational pull that keeps Him at the center of your being. You cannot isolate your children from the world, but you can teach them to recognize truth by keeping your family in orbit around the Son!

Basket of Beliefs

With five children under seven, my shelter constantly runs out of milk, bread, and snacks. At least three times a week my wife calls and asks me to stop by the grocery to pick up a few things on my way home. Invariably I run into someone I know. Each time this happens, I have an uncontrollable desire to look into his or her basket. Even if I try not to, I cannot help myself. I don't feel too badly about this because I notice without exception the person looks in my basket as well. So be careful about what you put in your basket!

When it comes to worldviews you must train yourself to keep an eye on everyone's basket of beliefs. As a parent you must beware of what you are putting in your basket as well as what your warriors are putting in theirs. It is not uncommon for Christ followers to try to put something in their basket of beliefs that Christianity simply will not pay for when it is time to check out!

Doppler Radar

The most effective tool meteorologists have to forecast severe weather is the WSR-88D, which stands for Weather Surveillance Radar - 1988 Doppler. These

Doppler radars are able to detect motion, using the Doppler effect. This ability to detect motion allows the meteorologist to measure what is happening inside a thunderstorm and determine if there is rotation in the cloud. This is crucial information because this rotation is usually the sign of a developing tornado. As the radar turns it emits pulses that last 0.00000157 seconds with a listening period that lasts 0.00019843 seconds. The radar is actually on for 7 seconds each hour and listens the remaining 59 minutes and 53 seconds.[5]

The radar listens for changes in pitch to determine if something is moving toward or away from the radar. If something is moving toward the radar it is recorded as a positive change. Likewise, if something is moving away from the radar it is recorded as a negative change. Did you notice how long the radar is actually sending out pulses? That's right, 7 seconds each hour. It spends the remaining 59 minutes and 53 seconds listening for signals. Parents have a lot to learn from Doppler radar!

Worldview Surveillance Radar

If God has placed a human soul under your responsibility then you need to function as Christian WSR. God expects parents to function as worldview surveillance radars as we do life with our kids. This is the essence of Deuteronomy chapter six. We are to detect when children are moving toward and away from truth. The idea is to send out pulses of truth and listen for signals from our children. We are commanded to carry this out from the time we wake up until the time we go to bed, while we are sitting in the living room, or driving down the road. God has consecrated dads and moms for the task of establishing a Christian worldview within their children. The goal is to help kids recognize truth and lead them to embrace it as such. You help

---

[5]http://www.srh.noaa.gov/jetstream/doppler/how.htm

them put the right stuff in their basket of beliefs. You also help them recognize the wrong stuff.

One evening I was watching television with my children and a commercial advertising a digital video recorder came on. The commercial featured the movie character Hellboy. My son Jonah rose up from the couch and yelled, "Dad, it's the devil! What are those things on his head?" I immediately responded in full WSR mode, "Boy that's not the devil. The Bible doesn't say anything about the devil having red skin, a goatee, and horns. Do you know what the Bible says about the Devil?" "What dad?" "The Bible says the devil presents himself as an angel of light. He looks very good and he lies all the time. If you don't understand what you believe you'll swallow a lie and process the wrong thing. You are warrior Jonah; you have to know the truth and that is not the truth about the devil." I communicated truth to my boys on their level, and then I had them repeat it to me. I don't want them growing up thinking the devil is a guy running around in a red suit tempting people. I want my kids to understand that he represents a force that opposes everything good God has created.

I am not following Christ because my parents are Christians. I am a Christ follower today because I have examined the evidence and I believe Christianity offers the best explanation for my existence! I want my kids to adopt the Christian worldview because it is true, not because our family worships at a Christian church. I think it is important to note that helping kids develop a Christian worldview does not necessarily ensure they are Christians. Each soul is responsible for surrendering his or her free will to Christ. That is a decision that must be made individually. But there is no doubt that helping kids develop a Christian worldview lays a foundation that enables them to recognize truth. If they are able to recognize the truth they will be set free from their sin.

To the Jews who had believed him,
Jesus said, "If you hold to my teaching, you
are really my disciples. Then you will know
the truth, and the truth will set you free"
(John 8:31-32).

Severe Storm Watch

The difference between a storm watch and a storm warning is simple; during a watch a severe storm could occur, during a warning a severe storm is occurring. Before leaving this chapter I want to advise you of two storms to watch out for. Occasionally I notice parents making a critical mistake while enforcing rules. A scenario such as a child wanting to engage in a behavior or wear an article of clothing that is not becoming of a Christian. The child questions the rule as to why they are not allowed to do this. The parent will then respond with "Because the Bible says so." While this may be true, it is a critical mistake in the development of a warrior's worldview. If kids grow up constantly being told they cannot do something because the Bible says so, then they will naturally grow to resent the Bible. Granted, it is much more difficult to help kids understand where something is taught in the Bible and why we are making this lifestyle decision, but God never said parenting was easy. Parenting is work and if you want your kids to develop a love for the Word of God then teach them to understand and appreciate it. Don't be lazy or you may be the one responsible for reinforcing their resentment toward the Bible.

Another storm parents must watch out for is the flood. Parents can spend too much time talking and not enough time listening. Too many times parents inundate their kids with truth. It is easy for a Christian parent to be so caught up with instilling truth that they bombard their children with it constantly. This flood of principles and deluge of comments can cause kids to tune out rather than absorb. It can also make parents think development is happening only when they are talking. Remember the Doppler radar transmits 7 seconds of each hour and listens for signals the other 59 minutes and 53 seconds.

Christian parents ought to be experts at listening for positive and negative signals from their children. If we listen more and learn to speak strategically there will be a lot less arguing and a lot more intentional development taking place. Ironically, Christian Doppler was the man responsible for discovering the Doppler effect. Are you a Christian Doppler?

Chapter 8

Brilliant Shelter

Developing for the Master

The Reward

If you want to live an incredible life you must have a vision for it. Life doesn't just happen. There is real danger in thinking that one day, eventually; something great will break for you. Greatness is not achieved overnight. Greatness is achieved day by day. If you can stack several successful days together then you'll have a great week. If you can stack up a few successful weeks, you can have a great month. If you can stack a few successful months together, you can have a great year. If you get this down and repeat the process until you die, you'll have a great life. A lot of people sit around waiting for the big break to happen. People who experience great lives don't sit around and wait for something to happen. Day by day they work hard at putting a great life together. So start building today!

It is extremely important to realize that what happens during your lifetime is eternally tied to your identity as a human being. You need to understand that there is a day coming when you will stand in judgment for your life. It will be a judgment regarding what you built with the life you lived. Life is basically a measurement of what you do with the time you are allotted to live. God expects you to use the time and experiences you are given to build something for Him. There are a lot of indifferent people who do not concern themselves with this reality at all. Then there are those who are consumed by it. That is what I want to challenge you to be; someone who is consumed with using your time and experiences to build eternally for God.

Incredible sacrifice, focus, and work are required to build people. If you leave this experience to chance you may end up with a pile of junk. On the other hand, if you commit to the correct process you can build something great for God and yourself. We are judged by what we build. To successfully construct a family shelter, you must commit to becoming an expert master builder. In his letter to the Corinthian Church the apostle Paul shared some fundamental principles that will enable us to build for eternity.

First Corinthians 3:9-17 has an incredible amount of both practical and theological application. It contains a convincing warning for Christ followers. Most Christians seem only to be aware of and show concern for The Great White Throne Judgment by which the saved and the lost are identified. Paul on the other hand, with tremendous urgency, notifies us that there is another judgment as well. It is evident that Paul is both warning of this impending judgment and explaining how to build for eternity.

Becoming an Expert Master Builder

When God gives us life He gracefully presents the opportunity to engage in eternal construction. The

Apostle Paul said, *For we are God's fellow workers; you are God's field, God's building. By the grace God has given me, I laid a foundation as an expert builder, and someone else is building on it* (1 Corinthians 3:9-10). The term *expert builder* comes from the Greek word *architekton*. It means superintendent or architect of a building project. We get our word *architect* from it. Paul is the superintendent of this particular project. He is the one God used to build the church at Corinth. Paul uses this metaphor to refer to the church, not a church building. The church is made up of people so he is communicating that he is an expert at building people. Paul sees himself as someone who helps other people become all God designed them to be.

He goes on to say he became an expert builder of people by the grace God gave to him. God's grace was poured over Paul's life and he became an *architekton*, a master builder of people. This is an incredible thought in and of itself, but notice what else Paul says. He says he laid a foundation but someone else is building on it. There are other people who are involved in this particular building project. The implication is that all believers are expected to build for God. You are either building something that brings glory to God or you are building something that takes glory away from God. You are either advancing the church or destroying the church with your life.

You build people starting with yourself. You work on yourself as you build your life upon the foundation of Jesus Christ. You work hard at building an incredible life for God by focusing on building people. This is the second part of the Great Commandment, which tells you to love your neighbor as yourself. You begin with your family by treating them the way God treats you. You build up your family for God and in so doing you construct a shelter that brings glory to Him.

Inside the protection of a family shelter parents build up children and children reciprocate by building up parents as well as their siblings. Human development takes place underneath the protection of a human shelter just like personal spiritual development takes place underneath the protection of a Divine Shelter. When this is achieved, it pours out of our experiences with our immediate families and touches our friends, loved ones, coworkers, and even the clerk at the service station. To live an incredible life you must spend your time and experiences building people, not careers, cash, cars, or castles.

If we would just discipline ourselves to begin each day with this truth it would revolutionize the way we live. Everyday we have an opportunity to build something great with and for God by utilizing our time and experiences! That is why I take time each morning to connect with God. I want to harmonize with what He is doing all around me. I want to be aware of this incredible opportunity I have to build a Shelter for Him. He has entrusted to my stewardship these amazing people I call my family. I get to develop these warriors and teach them how to connect with Christ and build up other people.

Rather than approaching life this way, many people wake in the morning to the sound of the alarm, thinking, "Here we go again; God, just help me get to Saturday." Or "Lord please help me make it another day. I can retire in ten more years and my life is going to be good." This is such a poor way to approach life. Your job may not be the greatest job on the planet but at least you are in a position to provide for your family. To build a great life you have to believe that God can use you to do something incredible each day. The first step to building something great for God is realizing that life is an extraordinary opportunity!

Building Carefully

As we continue to unpack this passage we learn that everyone should be careful because Jesus is the only foundation on which men can build eternal life experiences. *...But each one should be careful how he builds. For no one can lay any foundation other than the one already laid, which is Jesus Christ.*[1] These words of Scripture come alive as we imagine Paul emphatically warning, "Watch out, be careful!" You must be alert because Jesus Christ is not the only foundation on which you can build. Everyone is building, but not everyone is constructing for eternity. Everything that takes you away from the truth of Christ is junk. Everything that draws you into the truth of Christ is the kind of stuff to which you want to pay attention. There are two things true about every life experience you have. It either can or cannot be laid upon the foundation of Jesus Christ![1]

The danger within the western church is the compartmentalization of faith. Spiritual experiences are viewed as something that happens on the weekends as a religious observance. Work is work, entertainment is entertainment, education is education, and religion is religion. That is not the way Christianity is designed to operate at all. That is totally contrary to teaching of the New Testament. All of these relationships and experiences are to be laid before the throne of God and surrendered to Him. All of our life experiences are to be built upon the foundation of Jesus Christ. If you compartmentalize and just experience life by chance then you are not building for eternity; you are amassing a junk pile of experiences. That is precisely why Paul warns us to "BE CAREFUL!"

---

[1] 1 Corinthians 3:10-11

Selecting Building Material

There are a lot of materials in the world that can be used to build your life. But according to Paul all of it falls within two categories: permanent or perishable.[2] You must understand that building material does not necessarily have to be sinful to be perishable. People often pick good over better without realizing it. Jim Collins says in his book *Good to Great* that the worst enemy of greatness is good.[3] If you choose the wrong material, you may build something that looks incredible but looks can be deceiving. Over time the elements and storms that beat against your shelter will reveal whether or not you built an incredible life or a junk pile of experiences. Many people make decisions about life experiences with a sin test. For example, one might be inclined to participate in an activity because it is not a sin. This is a foolish way to approach life. First Corinthians 10:23 says, *Everything is permissible—but not everything is beneficial. Everything is permissible—but not everything is constructive.* Paul says he has tremendous freedom in Christ. But just because he can do certain things does not mean he should. The truth is, you can do a lot of things that are a complete waste of time because you are engaging in perishable experiences. Expert builders choose to construct life from permanent experiences. Look at your wife, children, business, recreation, and other life experiences and decide to build out of gold, silver, and precious stone.

View life as an incredible opportunity and choose permanent building materials because you know the foundation is worthy of such material. Avoid perishable experiences even though there may be nothing wrong with them. Learn how to choose great over good!

---

[2] 1 Corinthians 3:12
[3] 19 Collins, James C. ; *Good to Great: Why Some Companies Make the Leap and Others Don't*; HarperCollins Publishers, (2001).

Paul uses this metaphor because in his day there were two classes of society. There were the very rich and the very poor. It is difficult for Americans to wrap their minds around this because we have a middle class. I have been fortunate to travel to the Ivory Coast in West Africa and to Coahuila, Mexico. Both of these extremes exist in these two countries. You cannot help but notice these two extremes because what you observe are either mud huts or mansions. This is what Paul had in mind when he wrote this. Some homes were built with very precious material while others were built with wood, hay, and stubble.

Understand your financial situation has no bearing on your ability to build an incredible shelter for God. This is where I think many people are missing the mark when it comes to living a meaningful life. People are too caught up in living the American Dream and building mansions here at the expense of constructing mud huts for eternity. It is amazing to me that every single day God moves some how, some way, all around us. If you don't see God moving around you everyday it is because you are not paying attention. You are too caught up in perishable building material. The way to overcome this is to train yourself to ask what God is doing within the experiences you are having. If the answer is nothing you need to change your lifestyle!

Building Up to Code

If you have ever built anything inside city limits then you understand inspections and municipal codes. When you hire an electrician to wire your house, he has to rough it in and call for an inspection. Before you can install insulation and drywall the inspector must approve the electrical work. If your electrician's work does not meet code because of his methods or material you fail the inspection. It can be a very disappointing disruption to the project schedule. A lot of time is wasted because of shoddy work.

Paul is trying to prepare people for an imminent inspection.[4] This is not an inspection about whether or not you are allowed into heaven. It's about what you built while you were on earth. The blazing fire of Christ's final inspection will reveal your construction on earth. What you build with perishable material will go up in smoke. What you build with permanent material will be refined by fire. The permanent things you build will become more brilliant there than they are here. If you spend a lot of time building with perishable experiences it is going to be a very disappointing day for you. You may be saved but you will be disappointed!

I hear a lot of people say, "Well at least I'll be saved and get in." That is such a foolish statement and it lacks vision. Certainly you have seen victims interviewed on the news because they have lost their home to a storm or fire. Generally they say, "I am just glad everyone got out alive; we can rebuild." This inspection Paul is warning us about offers no opportunity for rebuilding. This life is it! What you are experiencing right now is it. When you stand before the Judgment Seat of Christ whatever survives His refining fire is what goes on into eternity. That is why it is so important to think about your life with an eternal perspective.

> *Don't you know that you yourselves are God's temple and that God's Spirit lives in you? If anyone destroys God's temple, God will destroy him; for God's temple is sacred, and you are that temple* (1 Corinthians 3:16-17).

We are building that which God lives in. What an incredible thought. We are the temple of God and our

---

[4] 20 1 Corinthians 3:13-15

experiences should be made up of eternal material instead of junk. We must open our spiritual eyes and behold what God is doing. God wants to do something incredible with your life right now. You are the temple of the Spirit of God. God will touch the people you touch. God will love the people you love. God will hear the people you hear. God lives in you!

Developing people for Christ on this side of eternity is an amazing experience. When your children embrace the truth of Christ and begin making decisions that bring glory to Him, you glow with pride. But you think you are proud now; just wait until your shelter passes through the refining fires of Christ. Everything you build out of permanent material on this side is brilliant on the other side. If you develop little warriors for Christ on this side, then you have an indescribable reward coming on the other side. Build your shelter with eternal material. Develop your children with permanent experiences and prepare yourself for the greatest day of your existence.

You are destined for a departure and a face-to-face meeting with Jesus Christ. Certainly this Day of Judgment will be intense. Imagine standing alone before all of creation and giving an account for the life you have lived. Many of our experiences will be perishable. Picture yourself standing before Jesus Christ alone, trembling as you watch all of your wasted experiences of perishable material go up in a consuming fire. Your eyes fill with tears as the charred stench of waste lingers in a thick low hanging cloud of smoke. You are broken, beaten, feeling empty, and weak. Then the Master says, "Rise to your feet." You feel yourself lifted by a power that you know well. With an outstretched arm Jesus says behold and all of creation observes beauty you are familiar with but are unable to recognize at this point. Then the beauty intensifies and it dawns on you as each of your warriors pass through the refining fire of Christ. All heaven erupts in applause as the King shouts, "Well done, master builder, brilliant shelter!"

The Reward

When life is over and time is no more,

Your body and soul unite on a distant but strangely familiar shore

You'll fall to your knees in humble disgust

As perishable experiences begin to combust

Your eyes fill with tears

As the air grows thick with the stench of wasted years

All is lost and you feel broke

As you fall on your face in a cloud of smoke

A tap on your shoulder and much to your surprise

You feel the gaze of grace from blazing eyes

You stand to your feet with great intent

To behold past experiences with the kids you were lent

Your warriors pass through one by one

As the Master exclaims, "Well done, Well done!"

– Jimmy Holbrook

Conclusion

I love the United States of America because it is the greatest country that has ever existed. But our culture is in a mess. I believe people are confused about morality and truth. As I see it, we can moan about the condition of society or we can wage a war to improve it. To win the battle we must have warriors who understand who God is and how much He loves this world. They must be equipped with truth and challenged to serve the King and His kingdom. If God has chosen you as a parent, He has entrusted an incredible responsibility to you. You pass on His values, character, and identity to the next generation.

It is a task that can leave a parent feeling overwhelmed. Be encouraged! You have what it takes! Even if you are a single parent going it alone or you are married to an unbeliever you can do this. One of my favorite verses says, "If God is for us who can be against us?" A divine call has been placed on your life to develop a warrior for Christ. We can change our culture by changing our families, starting with yours and mine.

We must enjoy our children while they are still children. They are changing before our very eyes. Each day that passes they talk a little better, laugh a little louder, run a little faster, and stay gone a little longer. We don't realize how fast they are growing and then they are gone. We have them throughout life but childhood is a gift. Resolve in your heart to soak it up for all it is worth. Play with them, hold them, love them, and develop them for Christ. You'll never regret it! Thanks for taking the journey with me. I can't wait to see your shelter shine on the other side!

LAUGHING IN THE MIDST OF MARRIAGE

LINDA ANN CROSBY

PRICE: **$10.99** 13-ISBN: 9780892655779

- A reminder for wives to laugh and have fun as they live out every rich, poor, sick, healthy, better, or worse vow.

- 52 short devotionals to help wives place their focus back on God, who is faithful to provide all they need.